MATHS PROBLEM SOLVING

FOOD

by Anita Loughrey

CONTENTS

INTRODUCTION

Context-based maths gives you a purpose for using maths, and cements your understanding of both why and how maths is applied to daily life. This book explores a range of numeracy skills and topics through 13 different real-life scenarios.

At the head of each section, there's a quick visual guide to the topic and skills covered. The introduction to each section sets the scene and presents the maths question that will be answered.

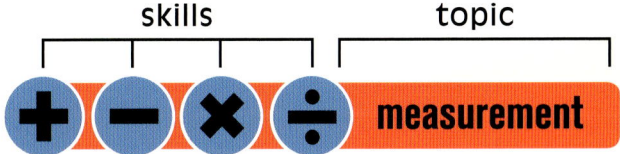

Then you are guided through the process of answering the question, step by step.

In addition, each section also contains helpful tips and an extra challenge: **Now try this ...**

There's an answer key for the **Now try this ...** challenge at the end of the book and words covered in the glossary are highlighted in **bold** throughout the text.

WHAT CAN YOU AFFORD FOR LUNCH?

You have £2.45 to spend on lunch. You could spend all your money on a jacket potato. Look at the menu and work out what else you can afford. First, how much would a salad and pizza cost?

> When working out the price of 2 or more items you need to add them up. A good written method for adding up numbers is column addition.

Menu

Jacket potato	£2.45
Salad	£1.10
Pizza	£1.35
Carrot sticks	£1.00
Fruit salad	£0.80
Juice	£0.65

There are 100 pennies in 1 pound. Write pounds in the hundreds column (H) and write pence in the tens (T) and units (U) columns.

Hundreds — Tens — Units

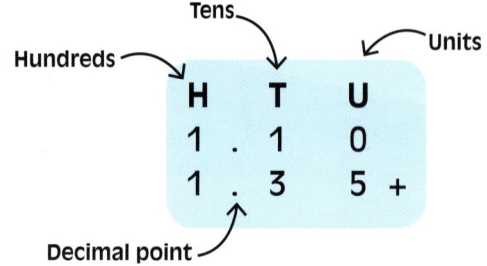

```
H   T   U
1 . 1   0
1 . 3   5 +
```

Decimal point

```
H   T   U
1 . 1   0
1 . 3   5 +
        5
```

Remember when doing column addition to always start with the numbers in the units column.

0 + 5 = 5

Write 5 in the units column answer box.

```
H   T   U
1 . 1   0
1 . 3   5 +
    4   5
```

Then add the numbers in the tens column.

1 + 3 = 4

Write 4 in the tens column answer box.

£1.10

£1.35

```
H   T   U
1 . 1   0   +
1 . 3   5
─────────
2 . 4   5
```

Last, add the numbers in the hundreds column.

1 + 1 = 2

Write 2 in the hundreds column answer box.

So, pizza and salad will cost you £2.45.

Here's another menu option. How much will it cost altogether?

£1   80p   65p

```
H   T   U
1 . 0   0   +
  . 8   0
  . 6   5
─────────
        5
```

0 + 0 + 5 = 5

Write 5 in the units column answer box. Then add the numbers in the tens column.

```
H   T   U
1 . 0   0   +
  . 8   0
  . 6   5
─────────
    4   5
1
```

0 + 8 + 6 = 14

Write 4 in the tens column answer box and carry over the 1 to the bottom of the hundreds column.

```
H   T   U
1 . 0   0   +
  . 8   0
  . 6   5
─────────
2 . 4   5
1
```

1 + 1 carried over = 2

Write 2 in the hundreds column answer box.

So, carrot sticks, fruit salad and a drink will also cost you £2.45.

You can also afford salad and pizza, or carrot sticks, fruit salad and a drink.

Make it easy!

There are 100 pennies in a pound.

A **decimal point** separates pounds from pence, e.g. £4.55. When **adding up** pounds and pence, line up the **decimal points** to make it easier.

Now try this ...

Your friend spends exactly £1.90. What does she choose from the menu?

HOW MUCH DOES A SLICE OF BREAD COST?

You're running the sandwich stall at your school fair. A large loaf of bread has 24 slices and costs £1.44. To give you an idea of how much to charge, you need to find out how much 1 slice of bread costs.

Sandwiches!

To work this out you have to divide the total cost by the number of slices. Remember £1.44 is the same as 144 pence (p).

This is your number sentence:
$144 \div 24 =$

Dividing is the opposite of multiplying and these numbers are in the 12 times table so you can use the 12 times table to work out the answer.

$12 \times 12 = 144$ which means $144 \div 12 = 12$.

12 is half of 24 so if $144 \div 12 = 12$ then $144 \div 24 = 6$.

This means each slice of bread costs 6 pence.

Let's check your answer ...

If you multiply the number of slices of bread by 6 pence, what do you get?

$24 \times 6 = 144$

 Each slice of bread costs 6p. Now you can start thinking about sandwich fillings!

Make it easy!

If you know all your **times tables** it is easy to work out **sums** in your head.

You can take out the **decimal point** when working out a **sum** to make it easier, but don't forget to put it back again at the end to get the answer in pounds.

Now try this ...

How many sandwiches can be made out of the loaf if we use two slices for each sandwich?

WHAT DO THE SCALES TELL YOU?

You are off school with a bad cold and your dad is going to make some of your favourite tomato soup. For this he needs 800 ml of stock and 450 g of tomatoes. He also wants to check your room is warm enough for you. It should be at least 21°C. Can you read the different **scales** to help him?

A measuring jug measures liquids. You measure liquids in litres (l) and millilitres (ml).

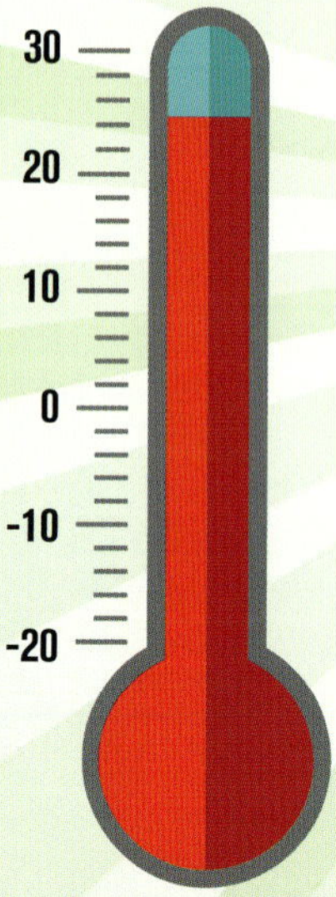

A thermometer measures temperature. You measure temperature in degrees Celsius (°C).

Weighing scales measures solids. You measure solids in grams (g) and kilograms (kg).

On the measuring jug you can see the water lines up exactly with the number 800 on the scale. This shows there is exactly 800 millilitres of water in the jug.

On the thermometer the line is halfway between 20 and 30. So you have to work out the small divisions on the scale.

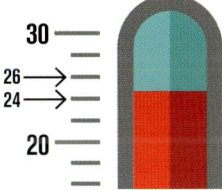

The scale between 20 and 30 degrees Celsius has been divided into 5 parts. There's a difference of 10 between 20 and 30 degrees Celsius.

$10 \div 5 = 2$

So each space on the scale represents 2°C.

But the line is exactly halfway between 24 and 26 degrees Celsius. So, the temperature must be 25 degrees Celsius.

On the weighing scales the arrow is halfway between 2 of the blue marks. The red division is exactly halfway between 0 and 200. To find out half of something, you divide it by 2.

$200 \div 2 = 100$

So the red marks each measure 100 grams. But what about the blue marks? There are 4 blue marks between each red mark. So you need to divide 100 by 4.

$100 \div 4 = 25$

Next, you need to look at the arrow again. It's just past the first red mark, so the tomatoes must weigh more than 100 grams. It is also past one blue mark, so they weigh 125 grams.

The scales tell you that there's enough stock to make your soup but you need more tomatoes, and that your room is just the right temperature!

Make it easy!

Always include the **units** you are working with, e.g. grams, degrees Celsius, litres, in your final answer.

Remember to work out the small **divisions** on the **scale** to make it easier.

Now try this ...

There are **negative numbers** at the bottom of the thermometer **scale**. How do you say these temperatures?

HOW MANY SWEETS ARE LEFT?

There are 42 sweets in the sweet jar in 7 different flavours. You eat all of the strawberry sweets. Your brother eats all of the banana sweets and all of the apple sweets. How many sweets are left now?

There's an equal number of each flavour so you can use fractions to help you work out how many sweets are left.

You ate all of 1 of the 7 flavours.
As a fraction that's $^1/_7$.

Your brother ate all of 2 of the 7 flavours.
As a fraction that's $^2/_7$.

When you add and subtract fractions the **denominator** (bottom number) stays the same. You only add or subtract the **numerator** (top number).

To work out how many sweets were eaten you have to add up the amount you ate and the amount your brother ate.

$^1/_7 + {}^2/_7 = {}^3/_7$

So, in total $^3/_7$ of the sweets were eaten.

To work out the number of sweets left, subtract the amount eaten from the total number there was at the start.

$^7/_7 - {}^3/_7 = {}^4/_7$

So $^4/_7$ of the sweets are left.

To work out the quantity of sweets that have been eaten you need to find out what $\frac{1}{7}$ of 42 is.

You can do this by dividing 42 by 7.

$42 \div 7 = 6$

This means that you ate 6 sweets. And because you ate all of one flavour, this means there are 6 sweets of each flavour.

Twice as many would be six doubled.

$6 + 6 = 12$ or $6 \times 2 = 12$

This means that your brother ate 12 sweets.

Again, to work out how many sweets were eaten in total you have to add up the amount you ate and the amount your brother ate.

$6 + 12 = 18$

So altogether 18 of the sweets were eaten.

Now subtract the amount eaten from the total number of sweets.

$42 - 18 = 24$

There are 24 sweets left. That's great news because even numbers can be shared equally

Make it easy!

Remember the **numerator** is the number at the top of the **fraction**. The **denominator** is the number at the bottom of the **fraction**.

Always double-check symbols in **sums**. A plus (+) means you're doing **addition** and a minus (−) means you're doing **subtraction**.

Now try this ...

32 more sweets are **added** to the sweet jar containing **24** sweets. You eat $\frac{3}{7}$ of the **total**. Your brother eats $\frac{2}{7}$. How many sweets are left?

HOW MUCH OF EACH INGREDIENT DO YOU NEED?

You are going to make some chocolate chip cookies.
Look at the ingredients you need to make 12 cookies.
How much of each ingredient will you need to make
6 cookies? And how about 18 cookies?

Chocolate chip cookies
(makes 12 cookies)

150 g plain flour

100 g butter

50 g sugar

50 g chocolate chips

First you have to decide which **operation** to use.
There may be some information in the question that
helps you to decide. The recipe serves 12 but you only
need to make enough for 6. Half of 12 is 6 so to do this
you have to halve the mixture.

When you halve a number you have to divide
it by 2. So you have to divide each of the
ingredients by 2.

Partition big numbers to make sums easier to do.

100 ÷ 2 = 50

50 ÷ 2 = 25

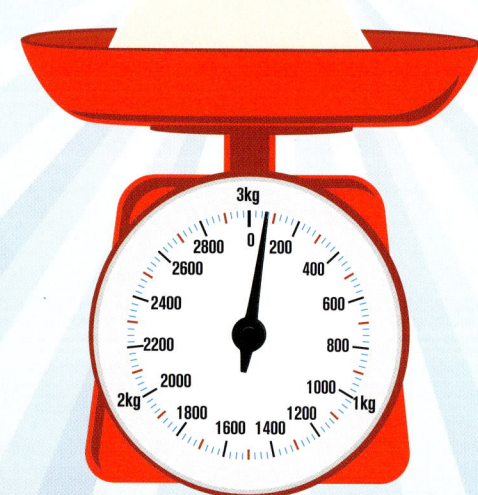

If half of 100 grams is 50 grams and half of 50 grams is 25 grams, you can add them together to work out what half of 150 grams is.

50g + 25g = 75g

So half of 150 grams is 75 grams.

To make 6 chocolate chip cookies you will need 75 grams of flour and 50 grams of butter.

Half of 50 is 25 so you need 25 grams of sugar and another 25 grams of chocolate chips.

Now how much of each ingredient would you need to make 18 cookies?

There are several ways you can work this out. 12 plus 6 makes 18 so you could add up the ingredients needed to make 6 and 12 cookies.

Flour	150 g + 75 g = 225 g
Butter	100 g + 50 g = 150 g
Sugar	50 g + 25 g = 75 g
Chocolate chips	50 g + 25 g = 75 g

6 times 3 is 18 so you could multiply the ingredients by 3.

Flour	75 g x 3 = 225 g
Butter	50 g x 3 = 150 g
Sugar	25 g x 3 = 75 g
Chocolate chips	25 g x 3 = 75 g

So, to make 6 cookies you'll need 75 g of flour, 50 g of butter, 25 g of chocolate chips and 25 g sugar. To make 18 cookies, you'll need 225 g of flour, 150 g of butter, 75 g of chocolate chips and 75 g of sugar.

Make it easy!

To **halve** a number, you **divide** it by two.

Half of 32 = 32 ÷ 2 = 16

Half of 16 = 16 ÷ 2 = 8

Half of 8 = 8 ÷ 2 = 4

Half of 4 = 4 ÷ 2 = 2

Doubling is the **opposite** of halving.

To **double** a number, you **multiply** it by two.

Double 3 = 3 x 2 = 6

Double 6 = 6 x 2 = 12

Double 12 = 12 x 2 = 24

Double 24 = 24 x 2 = 48

Now try this ...

You are going to make enough cookies for everyone in the class to have one.

There are 24 people including you and the teacher in your class.

How much of each ingredient would you need?

WHAT ARE THE PROPERTIES OF FOOD PACKAGING?

You want to make packaging for the food you're going to sell at the school fair. You'd like to work out the best shapes to use. But first what are the **properties** of different shaped packaging?

You can describe **3D shapes** by counting the number of faces, edges and vertices the shape has. These are known as their properties. Different shapes have different properties.

A **face** is a flat or curved surface.
- A cube has 6 flat surfaces
- A sphere has 1 curved face

An **edge** is the line where 2 surfaces meet.
- A cube has 12 edges
- A sphere has no edges

A **vertex** is a corner where 2 or more edges meet.
- A cube has 8 corners or vertices
- A sphere has no vertices

The cereal box is a 3D shape called a cuboid.

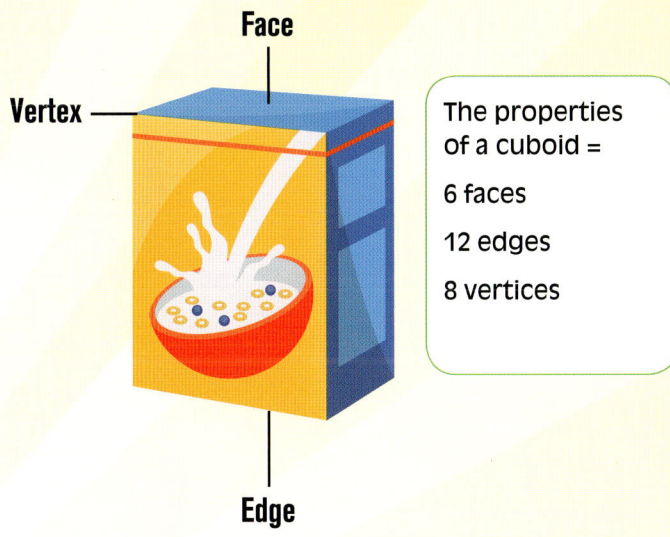

Face

Vertex

Edge

The properties of a cuboid =

6 faces

12 edges

8 vertices

The can of beans is a 3D shape called a cylinder.

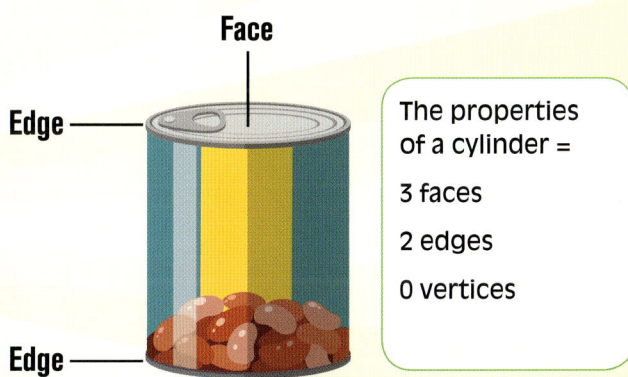

Face

Edge

Edge

The properties of a cylinder =

3 faces

2 edges

0 vertices

Property	Description	Shape	
		Cube	Sphere
face	flat or curved surface	6	1
edge	line where faces meet	12	0
vertex	corner or point	8	0

So now you know that packaging, like other 3D shapes, has faces and edges and sometimes vertices.

Make it easy!

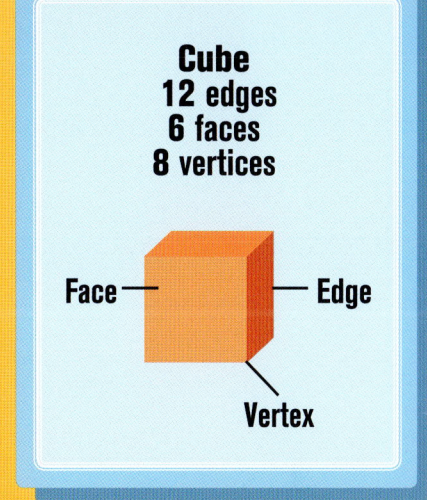

Cube
12 edges
6 faces
8 vertices

Face

Edge

Vertex

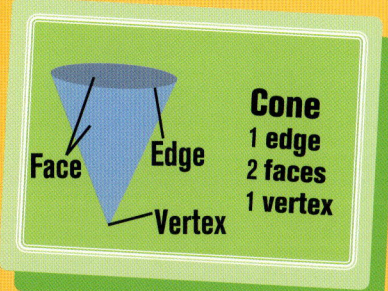

Face

Edge

Vertex

Cone
1 edge
2 faces
1 vertex

Now try this ...

Sandwiches bought in a supermarket are often in packaging shaped like a **rectangular-based pyramid**. What are the **properties** of a **rectangular**-based pyramid?

HOW MUCH PORRIDGE COULD MY CLASS EAT IN A WEEK?

There are 36 children in your class. On Monday morning, all of you told your teacher what you had eaten for breakfast. Then she put the data in a **bar chart**. Can you use it to find out exactly how many more children ate cereal than fruit, and how many bowls of porridge your class might eat in a week?

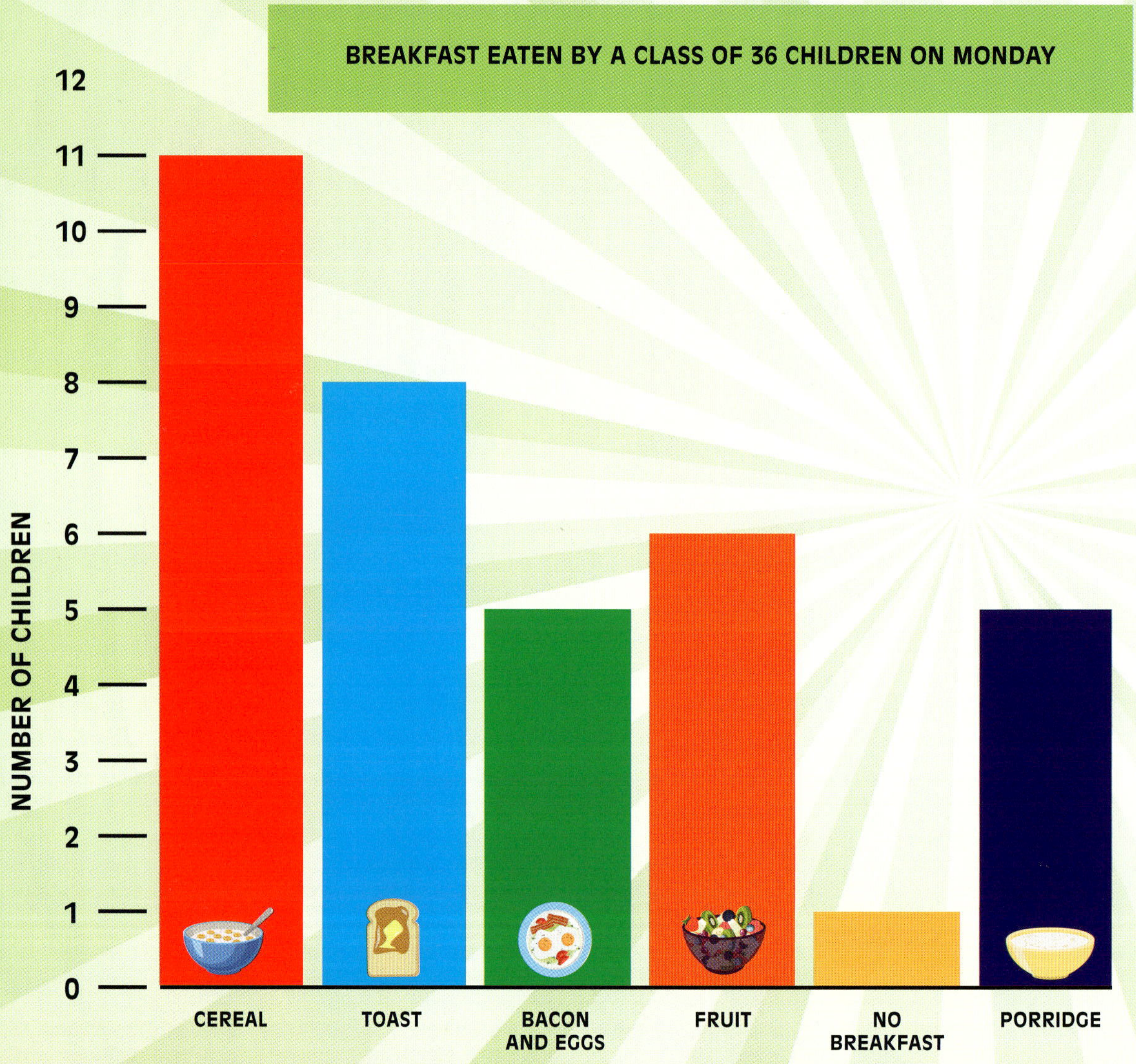

BREAKFAST EATEN BY A CLASS OF 36 CHILDREN ON MONDAY

NUMBER OF CHILDREN

	CEREAL	TOAST	BACON AND EGGS	FRUIT	NO BREAKFAST	PORRIDGE
Value	11	8	5	6	1	5

You can see how many children ate cereal by reading the number at the top of the column labelled CEREAL. It shows 11 children ate cereal.

How many more children had cereal than fruit?

To find this out, you have to subtract the amount of children who ate fruit from the number who ate cereal.

11 − 6 = 5

Five more children ate cereal than ate fruit on Monday morning.

Subtracting a smaller number from a larger number will always tell you the difference between them.

If the children ate the same breakfast every day for a week, how many bowls of porridge would they have eaten in total?

You can see 5 bowls of porridge were eaten on Monday. You also know there are 7 days in a week.

5 x 7 = 35

Now try this ...

How many children **in total** ate hot food for breakfast?

Five more children ate cereal than fruit and your class might eat 35 bowls of porridge in 1 week.

17

HOW MUCH SUGAR IS IN ONE SERVING OF POPCORN?

You've decided to limit the amount of sugar you eat to 15 grams per day. Food packaging usually has a chart showing its nutritional value. Sometimes the information is confusing. Can you find out if you can eat one serving of popcorn every day?

Toffee popcorn

175 g

Typical values per 100g

Energy	Fat	Saturates	Sugars	Salt
419 kcal	14 g	7.5 g	56 g	3.7 g

Suggested serving 25 g

The suggested serving for toffee popcorn is 25 g but the packet contains 175 g.

So how many servings does the whole bag of popcorn contain?

To work out how many servings are in the whole packet of toffee popcorn you have to divide 175 by 25.

You can make this easier by working out how many sets of 25 go into 100 and then how many go into 75.

You can use a method called **chunking** to do this. Chunking is a way of dividing numbers into chunks to make them easier to calculate with.

25 + 25 + 25 = 75

25 + 25 + 25 + 25 = 100

So now you know there are 3 groups of 25 in 75. And there are 4 groups of 25 in 100.

3 + 4 = 7

This means there are 7 groups of 25 in 175.

So there are 7 servings in a 175 g bag of toffee popcorn.

The information on the packaging tells us there are 56 g of sugar in 100 g of popcorn. So how much sugar is there in one 25 g serving?

We can work this out by dividing 56 by 4.

56 ÷ 4

To work out how many fours there are in 56, we can halve 56 and then halve it again.

It will make 56 easier to deal with if you split it into two chunks:

56 = 50 + 6

Half of 50 is 25. Half of 6 is 3.
Add them together:

25 + 3 = 28

So half of 56 is 28.

What's half of 28?

14!

Now we know there are 14 fours in 56. So there are 14 grams of sugar in 1 serving of popcorn.

Great news! There are 14 g of sugar in 1 serving of toffee popcorn so you can have 1 serving each day.

Make it easy!

You can make your own **times tables** to work out how many times smaller numbers go into bigger numbers.

Chunk difficult numbers into easy numbers before starting sums. 129 can be chunked into 100, 20, 5 and 4.

Now try this ...

How much sugar is there in the whole bag of toffee popcorn?

WHICH MULTIPACK IS THE BEST VALUE?

You take a bottle of orange juice to school every day. It's cheaper to buy a multipack than individual bottles. Multipacks are sold in packs of 4 or 8. But which multipack is the best value for money and by how much?

First you need to work out the price of 1 bottle of orange juice in each of the multipacks. So you need to divide the price by the number of bottles in the pack.

You can use the bus stop method to work out the price of 1 bottle for each of the multipacks.

Start with the pack of 4. You need to divide £2.48 (or 248p) by 4.

$$4 \overline{)\ 248\ }$$

You can't divide 2 by 4, so you need to try dividing 24 by 4.

$$\begin{array}{r} 6 \\ 4 \overline{)\ 248\ } \end{array}$$

Now divide 8 by 4 to get your answer.

$$\begin{array}{r} 62 \\ 4 \overline{)\ 248\ } \end{array}$$

So, 1 bottle of orange juice from the multipack of 4 costs 62p.

£2.48

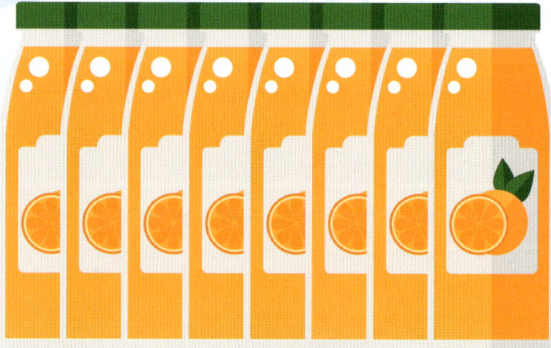

£3.60

Now you need to use the bus stop method to work out how much 1 bottle from the pack of 8 costs.

$$8 \overline{)\ 360}$$

You can't divide 3 by 8 so you have to try and divide 36 by 8.

If you know the 8 times table, you'll know 8 goes into 32 four times.

$$8 \overline{)\ \overset{4}{360}}$$

But there's a remainder of 4. Write 4 next to the zero so that it reads 40.

$$8 \overline{)\ \overset{4}{36^{4}0}}$$

8 goes into 4 five times so:

$$8 \overline{)\ \overset{45}{36^{4}0}}$$

So now you know that each bottle of juice in the pack of 8 costs 45 pence.

That means that the 8-bottle multipack is the best value for money.

To work out the difference in the price of a single bottle from the 4 pack and the 8 pack, subtract the lower price from the higher price:

62p – 45p = 17p

The multipack of 8 is cheaper than the multipack of 4 by 17 pence per bottle.

Multipacks of 8 are definitely the best value for money.

Make it easy!

Remove the decimal point and work out the **sum in pence** to make it easier.

£2.48 = 248p
£3.60 = 360p
£1.76 = 176p
£3.87 = 387p

Knowing your **times tables** always helps with the **bus stop method.**
Practise them every day - especially the ones you find difficult!

Now try this ...

The pack of 4 bottles is on sale at £1.76 and a new 8 bottle multipack is available for £3.87.

Which of the 3 multipacks is the best value for money now?

ARE YOUR BAGS ROUGHLY THE SAME WEIGHT?

You are helping your brother with the shopping. You want to load the shopping into two bags that weigh roughly the same. Can you do it?

500 g

SUGAR

1.5 kg

1 kg

FLOUR

250 g

100 g

3 kg

To work this out, it will help to **convert** all the weights to grams.

1 kilogram is the same as 1,000 grams. So, 3 kilograms is the same as 3,000 grams. And half a kilogram is 500 grams.

0.5 is the same as half. This means that 1.5 kilograms is the same as 1 ½ kilograms, or 1,500 grams.

Now you can put the different shopping items in order, from the heaviest to the lightest.

Potatoes	3,000 g
Flour	1,500 g
Sugar	1,000 g
Cereal	500 g
Apples	250 g
Tomatoes	100 g

Next you need to organise them into 2 groups of a similar weight. Start by looking at your heaviest item – the potatoes at 3,000 grams – and adding up the next heaviest items so that they match this weight:

1,500 + 1,000 = 2,500

2,500 + 500 = 3,000

So, now you know that if you put the flour, sugar and cereal in one bag and the potatoes in the other, each bag will weigh the same.

The apples and tomatoes aren't the same weight but if you put the apples in one bag and the tomatoes in the other, the bags will weigh roughly the same.

 Yes! By putting the potatoes and the tomatoes in one bag and the rest of the shopping in the other, you'll have two bags that weigh roughly the same. And hopefully there will be no arguing over who's got the heaviest bag!

Make it easy!

Convert numbers to the same unit of measurement to compare them easily:

1 kg = 1000 g
500 g = 500 g
0.25 kg = 250 g

Learn equivalent decimals and fractions to help you calculate quickly:

½ = 0.5
¼ = 0.25
¾ = 0.75

Now try this ...

If you had three bags and your potatoes weighed 2,000 g, how would you fill them so they weighed roughly the same?

HOW MANY LITRES OF SOUP DOES YOUR AUNT MAKE?

Your aunt runs a café and she makes the tastiest vegetable soup ever. A soup bowl holds 500 millilitres of soup. Your aunt makes enough for 16 bowls. Can you work out how many litres she makes each day?

You could multiply 500 millilitres by 16 but that seems a little difficult.

It is easier if you convert millilitres (ml) into litres (l).

500 ml = ½ l

Now you know that 1 bowl contains half a litre of soup, it's easy to work out that 2 bowls contain 1 litre of soup. What operation can you use to work out what 16 bowls contain?

An easy calculation would be to divide 16 by 2.

16 ÷ 2 = 8

 So your aunt makes 8 litres of vegetable soup each day.

Make it easy!

Liquids are measured in **litres** and **millilitres**
½ l = 500 ml
1 l = 1,000 ml

The **inverse operation** of **division** is **multiplication**.

Now try this ...

The next day your uncle makes 9 litres of lentil soup.

How many bowls of lentil soup can be served?

WHEN WILL LUNCH BE READY?

Lunch was put in the oven at 10.30 a.m. It takes 2 hours and 45 minutes to cook. You are already hungry and you want to work out when it will be ready!

You need to add the cooking time of 2 hours and 45 minutes to 10.30 a.m. First partition time to make it easier to calculate your answer.

10.30 is 10 hours and 30 minutes and you want to add 2 hours and 45 minutes to them.

First add the hours together:

10 + 2 = 12

(So lunch won't be ready before midday!)

Then add the minutes:

30 + 45 = 75

Remember! There are 60 minutes in an hour so 75 minutes is the same as 1 hour and 15 minutes.

So, now add 1 hour and 15 minutes to 12:

12 hours + 1 hour + 15 minutes = 13 hours 15 minutes

As a time, 13 hours 15 minutes is written as 13:15 on the 24 hour clock. To know the time on a 12 hour clock, we have to take away 12:

13.15 – 12.00 = 1.15

So, lunch will be ready at 1.15 pm. Now you need to work out if you're

Make it easy!

1 hour = 60 minutes
½ hour = 30 minutes
¼ hour = 15 minutes
¾ hour = 45 minutes

a.m.
after midnight and before midday

p.m.
after midday and before midnight

Now try this ...

What time would the meal be ready if it was put in the oven at half past two in the afternoon? What time would this be on the 24 hour clock?

CAN YOU AFFORD THE PARTY FOOD?

You are planning a birthday party for 12 friends. You have a budget of £40. You've written a shopping list and now you want to work out if you can afford everything.

Food	Veggie bites	Bread sticks	Sausages	Juice	Jelly	Pizza
Number in pack	36	24	12	12	6	1
Price per pack	£3.00	£2.40	£1.75	£4.25	£1.65	£1.20
Number needed	1	1	1	2	2	12

The total costs for veggie bites, bread sticks and sausages don't need to be totalled up as you're only buying one packet of each.

You can calculate juice easily: £4.25 x 2 = £8.50

You can calculate how much 2 packs of jelly costs by multiplying £1 by 2 and then 65p (£0.65) by 2:

£1 x 2 = £2
£0.65 x 2 = £1.30

Add these together and you have the total for jelly:

£2 + £1.30 = £3.30

You can calculate how much 12 packs of pizza costs by multiplying £1.20 by 10 and then £1.20 by 2:

£1.20 x 10 = £12
£1.20 x 2 = £2.40

Add these together and you have the total for pizza:

£12 + £2.40 = £14.40

Then add all your totals together to find out the final total amount.

Prices with pence that add up to one pound or less are easy to add together:

Pizza and veggie bites   £14.40 + £3.00 = £17.40

Pizza, veggie bites and jelly   £17.40 + £3.30 = £20.70

Juice and bread sticks   £8.50 + £2.40 = £10.90

Next add the pounds:

£20 + £10 = £30

And then add the pence:

£0.70 + £0.90 = £1.60

Yes! The party food will cost you £31.60 so you'll have some change left over. What will you spend it on?

Make it easy!

Use **partitioning** to make **adding decimals** easier.

£20.70 = £20 + 0.70
£10.90 = £10 + 0.90
£14.40 = £14 + 0.40

When you are **adding up** lots of numbers, add numbers that **total** less than ten first as you don't have to **carry** them **over** to the next **column**.

Now try this ...

The birthday cake costs £5.50. How much change do you have left now?

GLOSSARY

3D shape A three-dimensional shape, e.g. a cone, cube, cuboid, cylinder, pyramid or sphere.

Bar chart A chart that displays data using rectangular bars of different heights.

Chunking A method used for dividing large numbers by working out how many groups of numbers will go into a number.

Convert To change a unit of measurement e.g. weight can be changed from kilograms (kg) to grams (g); capacity can be changed from litres (l) to millilitres (ml). We can also convert fractions into decimals and decimals into fractions.

Decimal point A small dot that separates the whole number from the fractions of a number, as used when working with money to separate the pounds from the pence e.g. £3.56.

Denominator The bottom number of a fraction, e.g. the denominator of ½ is 2.

Edge The line where two faces meet in a 3D shape.

Equivalent The same as. Equivalent fractions are fractions that are the same amount as each other e.g. ½ is the same as ²/₄. Equivalent decimals are numbers with a decimal point that are the same as a fraction e.g. 0.5 is the same as ½.

Face The flat surface of a 3D shape. A sphere has a curved face.

Inverse operation The opposite operation, e.g. addition is the inverse of subtraction; multiplication is the inverse of division, doubling is the inverse of halving.

Negative numbers Numbers below zero. We write negative numbers with a minus sign, e.g. -5.

Numerator The top number of a fraction, e.g. the numerator of ¾ is 3.

Operation The four mathematical operations are addition (+), subtraction (-), multiplication (x) and division (÷).

Partition To separate numbers into thousands, hundreds, tens and units to make calculations easier.

Properties Words that describe 3D shapes, e.g. faces, edges and vertices.

Scale The unit of measurement to show the quantity of something. The scale on a ruler is in centimetres (cm) and millimetres (mm); the scale on weighing scales is in kilograms (kg) and grams (g); the scale on a jug is in litres (l) and millilitres (ml); the scale on a thermometer is in degrees Celsius (°C).

Vertex (plural: **vertices**) The point where two or more edges meet in 3D and 2D shapes.

NOW TRY THIS ... ANSWERS

Page 5
She buys a salad and some fruit salad.
£1.10 + 80p = £1.90

Page 7
24 ÷ 2 = 12

Page 9
-1 (degrees Celsius)
for example

Page 11
For the new total amount of sweets:
32 + 24 = 56
56 ÷ 7 = 8
$\frac{1}{7}$ = 8
For the new total amount of sweets eaten by you and your brother:
$\frac{3}{7} + \frac{2}{7} = \frac{5}{7}$ and then 8 x 5 = 40
For the new total amount of sweets left afterwards:
56 – 40 = 16
There are 16 sweets left.

Page 13
We need to double all the ingredients in the original recipe.
150 g x 2 = 300g of flour
100 g x 2 = 200g of butter
50 g x 2 = 100g of sugar
50 g x 2 = 100g of chocolate chips

Page 15
A rectangular based pyramid has 9 edges, 5 faces and 6 vertices.

Page 17
8 children ate toast, 5 ate bacon and eggs and 5 ate porridge.
8 + 5 + 5 = 18
18 children ate hot food for breakfast.

Page 19
There are 14 g of sugar in 1 serving and there are 7 servings in 175 g packet.
14 x 7 = 98
There are 98 grams of sugar in the whole bag of popcorn.

Page 21
£1.76 ÷ 4 = 44p
£3.87 ÷ 9 = 43p
It is cheaper to buy the multipack of 9.

Page 23
Bag 1: potatoes = 2,000 g
Bag 2: flour (1,500 g) and apples (250 g) = 1,750 g
Bag 3: sugar (1, 000 g), cereal (500 g) and tomatoes (100 g) = 1,600 g

Page 25
9 x 2 = 18
18 bowls of lentil soup can be served.

Page 27
2.30 + 2 hours = 4.30
4.30 + 45 minutes = 5.15
5.15 + 12 hours = 17.15

Page 29
£40.00 – £31.60 = £8.40
£8.40 – £5.50 = £2.90
You'll have £2.90 left in change.

Published in paperback in Great Britain in 2020 by Wayland
Copyright © Hodder and Stoughton, 2018
All rights reserved

Produced for Wayland by Dynamo
Written by: Anita Loughrey

ISBN: 978 1 5263 0795 8

Wayland, an imprint of
Hachette Children's Group
Part of Hodder and Stoughton
Carmelite House
50 Victoria Embankment
London EC4Y 0DZ

An Hachette UK Company
www.hachette.co.uk
www.hachettechildrens.co.uk

Printed in China

10 9 8 7 6 5 4 3 2 1